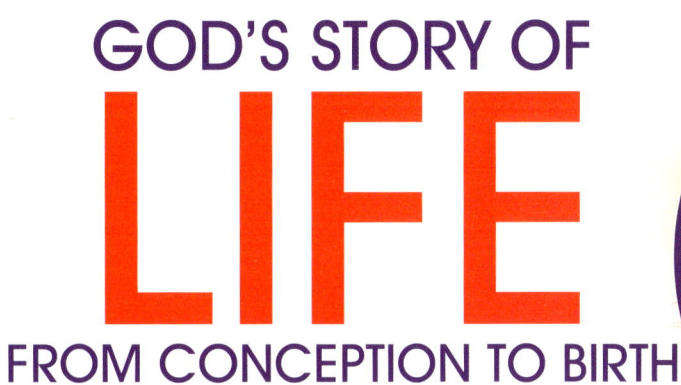

# WONDERFULLY MADE
## GOD'S STORY OF
# LIFE
### FROM CONCEPTION TO BIRTH

### Danika Cooley
#### ILLUSTRATED BY JEFF ANDERSON

CF4·K

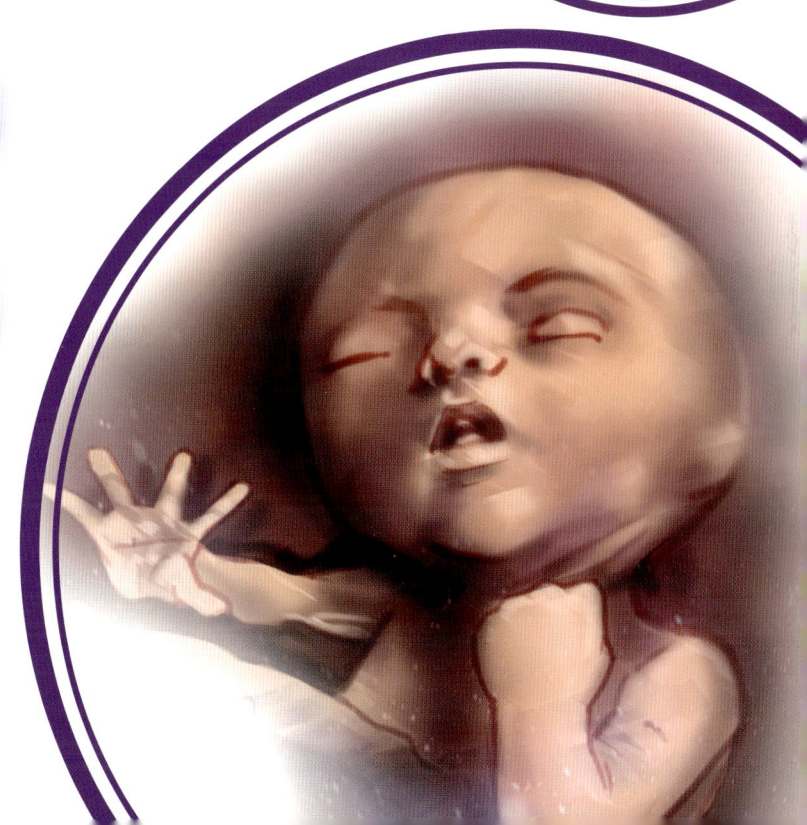

Author's Dedicaton: To Amber and Tyson, who grew in my heart, and to Forrest and Erik, who God formed within me.

10 9 8 7 6 5 4 3 2 1
Copyright © 2016 Danika Cooley
ISBN: 978-1-78191-678-0
Published in 2016 by Christian Focus Publications Ltd.
Geanies House, Fearn, Tain, Ross-shire, IV20 1TW, Great Britain
Illustrations by Jeff Anerson
Pete Barnsley (Creative Hoot)
Printed in China

All rights reserved. No part of this publication may be reproduced, stored in a retrieval system, or transmitted, in any form, by any means, electronic, mechanical, photocopying, recording or otherwise without the prior permission of the publisher or a licence permitting restricted copying. In the U.K. such licences are issued by the Copyright Licensing Agency, Saffron House, 6-10 Kirby Street, London, EC1 8TS. www.cla.co.uk

Scripture quotations are from The Holy Bible, English Standard Version, copyright © 2001 by Crossway Bibles, a division of Good News Publishers. Used by permission. All rights reserved. ESV Text Edition: 2007.

*Danika Cooley captures the wonder of our creation ... This is a great book for an expecting parent to read to their expecting children.*
LAINNA CALLENTINE, M.ED., M.D. PEDIATRICIAN AND AUTHOR

# Given with love to: ...................................

# From: ............................................................

Sit down with me, little one, and I'll tell you again how you grew inside of me. I loved your dad very much. He and I promised to love and care for each other our entire lives in an important ceremony before God. All our friends and family came to be witnesses to the special love God gave us.

The Lord made a way for a husband and wife to join together to show their special love and to create a baby.

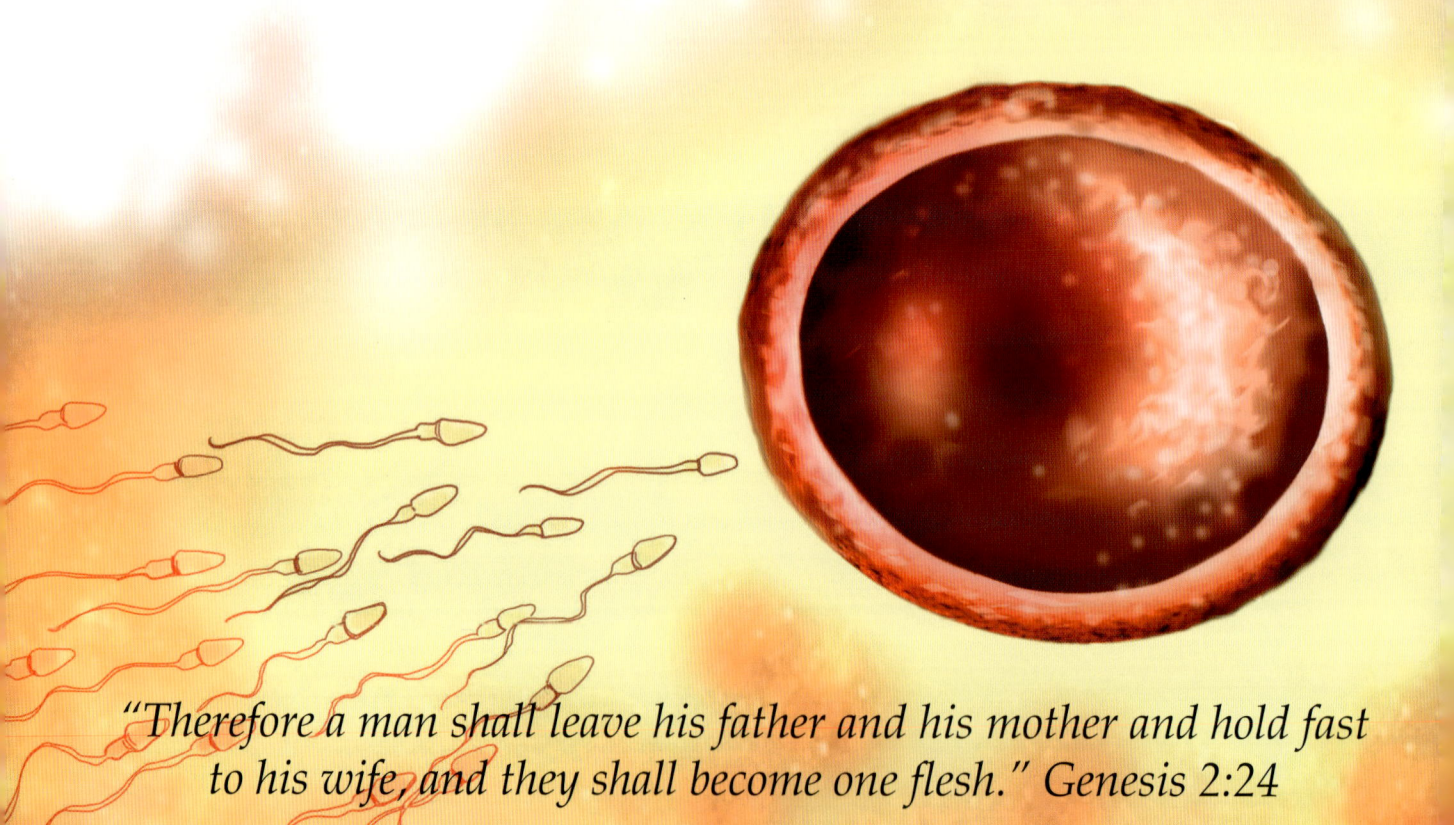

*"Therefore a man shall leave his father and his mother and hold fast to his wife, and they shall become one flesh." Genesis 2:24*

The doctor told me I would be pregnant for forty weeks. On weeks One and Two you weren't created yet, but God knew who you were going to be!

When your dad and I joined together to show the special love we have as a husband and wife, a cell from your dad, called a sperm, was able to swim to a cell in me, called an egg. Your life began in week Three, when one of my egg cells combined with one of Dad's sperm cells. Each cell had a blueprint for who you would be.

*"Before I formed you in the womb I knew you..." Jeremiah 1:5a*

The two blueprints combined, so you were born a little like me and a little like Dad. God had already recorded your hair, eye and skin color!

Three days later, that one cell had divided into nine cells, each with the same blueprint. You traveled down a long, dark tube into the middle of one of the most amazing muscles in my whole body: my womb.

You were tiny; the size of the head of one of my silver sewing pins.

By the end of week Four, big changes were occurring! You were smaller than a grain of rice, but your heart was beating.

You were busy growing a brain, skin, hair, skeleton, muscles, liver, pancreas and digestive and blood systems. What a miracle it was!

*"Did you not pour me out like milk and curdle me like cheese? You clothed me with skin and flesh, and knit me together with bones and sinews?" Job 10:11*

You kept growing in weeks Five and Six. Now you were a little bigger than a nail head.

God surrounded you in a liquid called amniotic fluid. You were protected and nourished in this amazing solution until you were born. You had leg and arm buds with little paddles for hands. Small bumps appeared where your nose, eyes and ears were growing. A thin layer of see-through skin covered your whole body.

The heart beating inside of you looked like a tube. Your spinal cord was forming, and so was your brain. Your digestive system was growing, but it was not ready for food yet.

To tell the truth, you looked a little like a tadpole; you even had a tail! You didn't look like that for long, though. God had a plan.

You were getting bigger every day! In week Seven, your tail was disappearing and your neck was starting to show. Your legs looked like small fins. God was growing your arms and you had visible hands and shoulders. Your heart no longer looked like a tube; it had right and left chambers and it didn't quite fit all the way in your chest. In fact, it was only protected by your thin skin. Your intestines were growing and bulged out of your body, too.

*"Behold, you delight in truth in the inward being, and you teach me wisdom in the secret heart." Psalm 51:6*

By week Eight, big things had happened! You were the size of a pencil sharpener. You weren't ready to be born yet, but now I knew you were there.

This week, you had elbows, eyelids and fingers, called digital rays. Your nose tip and your ears were being formed. Your body was growing straighter.

All of your internal organs were working, except for your lungs. God waited until the very end to finish forming the sacs that help you breathe.

This week we saw a picture of you on a machine called an ultrasound. What a teeny, tiny, wonderful baby you were!

By week Nine, you were the size of a green olive. Your arms, legs, feet and fingers were longer and you liked to put your hands close together over your heart. Your neck had grown and your head was off your chest. God was almost done forming little ears and eyelids. You were making faces and moving your body!

Though God always knew whether you were a boy or a girl, now your body showed it too.

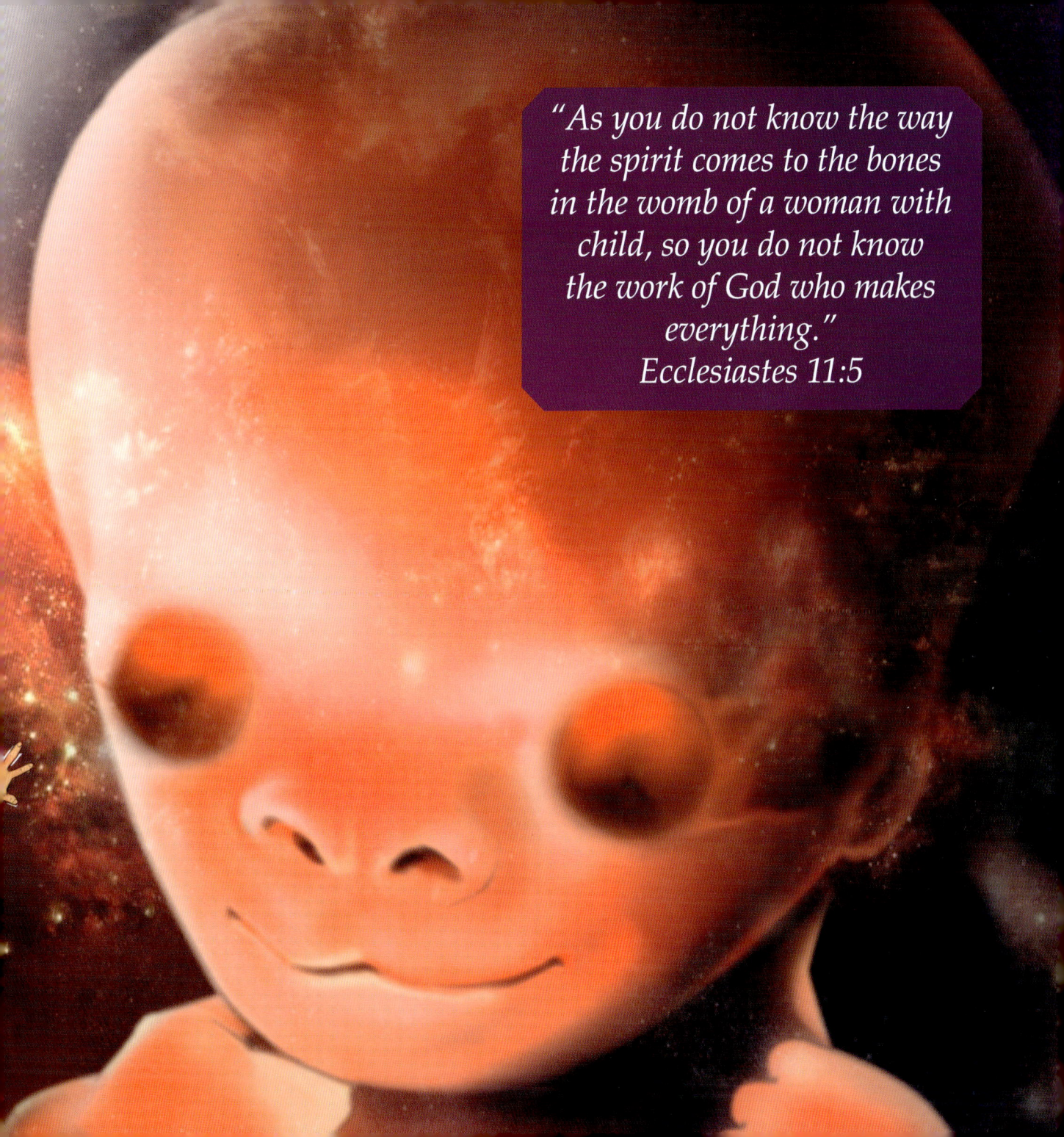

"As you do not know the way the spirit comes to the bones in the womb of a woman with child, so you do not know the work of God who makes everything."
Ecclesiastes 11:5

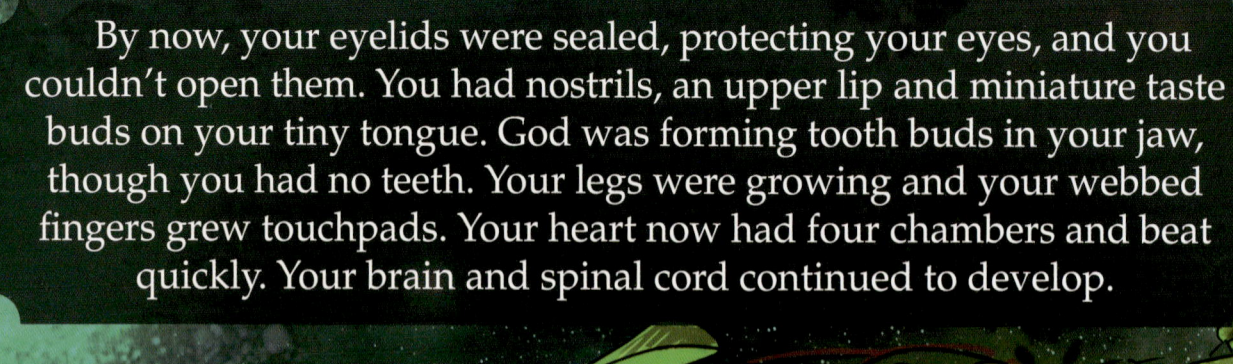

My child, in week Ten, you were the size of a small plum. You and I were connected by an umbilical cord that circulated blood.

By now, your eyelids were sealed, protecting your eyes, and you couldn't open them. You had nostrils, an upper lip and miniature taste buds on your tiny tongue. God was forming tooth buds in your jaw, though you had no teeth. Your legs were growing and your webbed fingers grew touchpads. Your heart now had four chambers and beat quickly. Your brain and spinal cord continued to develop.

Your muscles were almost all where they were supposed to be, and you were practicing moving in the amniotic fluid.

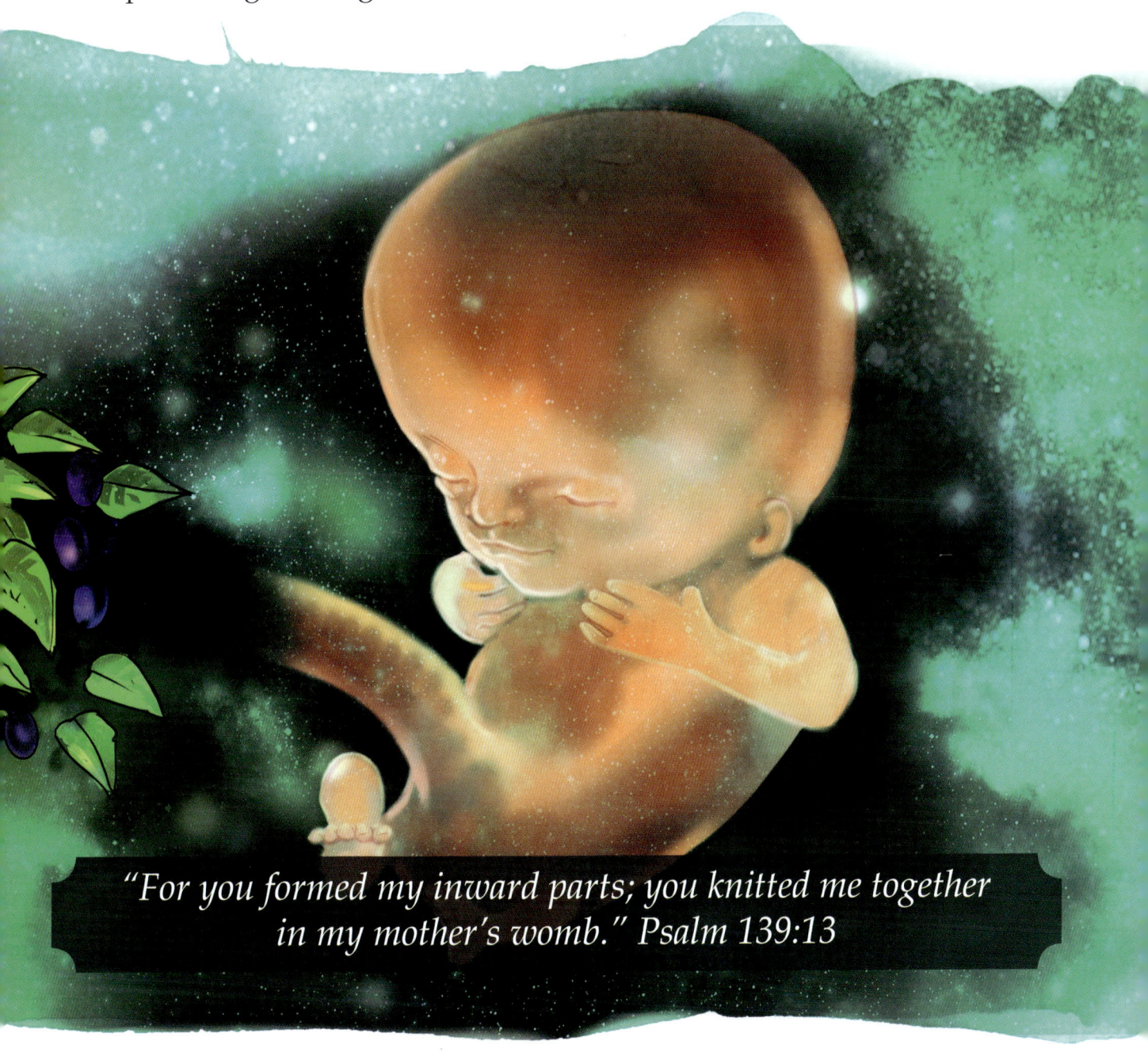

"For you formed my inward parts; you knitted me together in my mother's womb." Psalm 139:13

By week Eleven, you had been growing inside me for nine whole weeks. You were the size of a large lime!

Our Heavenly Father had formed your face. Your eyes and ears were fully developed. Fine hairs covered your see-through skin. Your fingers and toes were separating and your fingernails were growing.

God had big plans for you, little one. Now all your major organs were in place and by week Twelve, you were practicing the important things you would need to do to live outside of me.

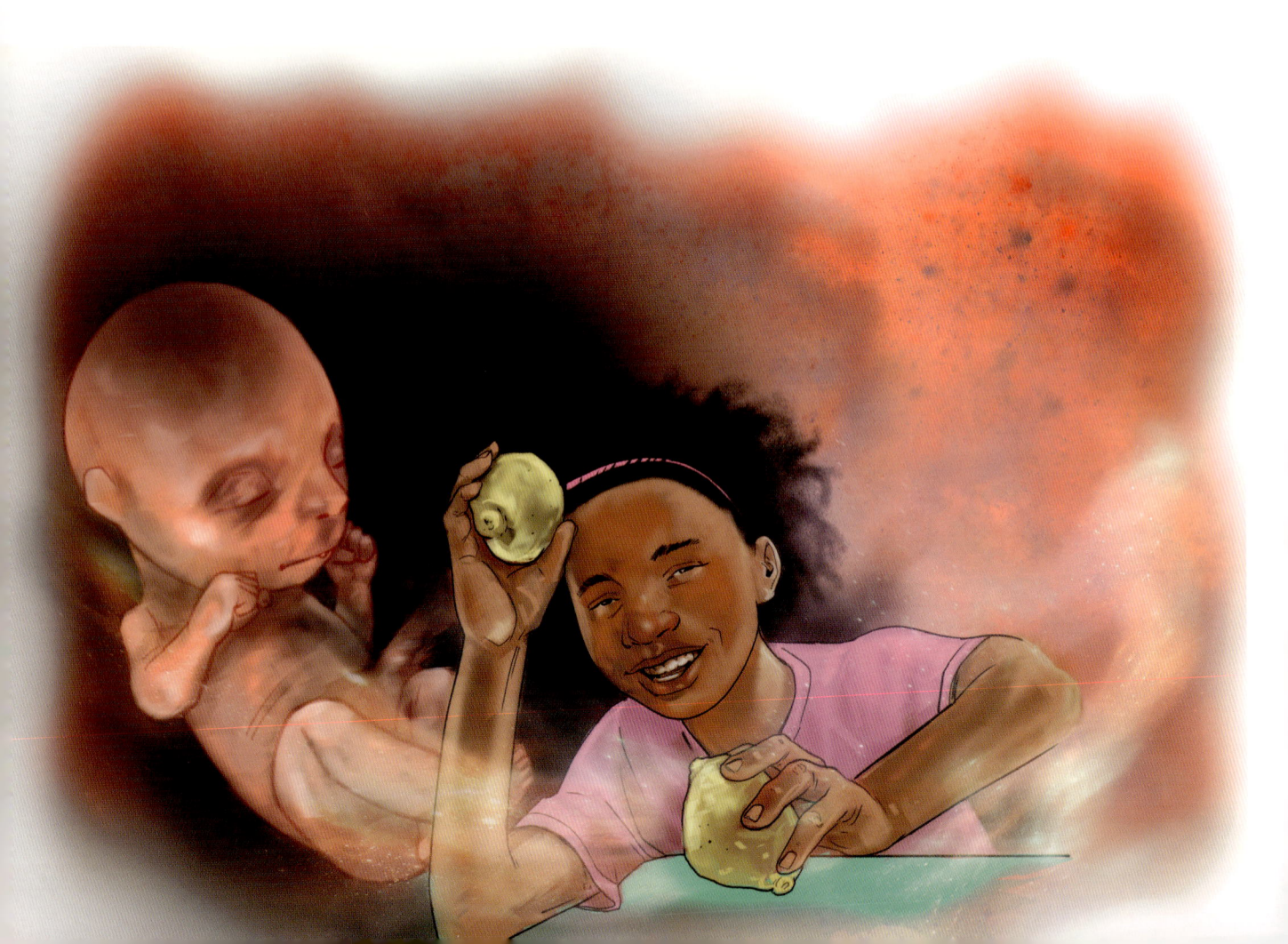

You moved in quick little jerks. Your chest muscles were growing stronger; you practiced breathing the fluid you were swimming in. You swallowed the fluid as well and sometimes, you got the hiccups! Your liver started making blood cells and your small intestines contracted and absorbed sugar.

The soft cartilage of your skeletal system was hardening to bone. In fact, it won't be done hardening until you are grown.

You would have been fun to watch; you were opening your mouth, waving your little fingers and toes and squinting when it was too bright.

> " *I praise you, for I am fearfully and wonderfully made. Wonderful are your works; my soul knows it very well.*" Psalm 139:14

By week Thirteen you were huge: the size of an apple or a peach! Now your body was growing faster than your head and your heart beat had slowed. Your intestines were sinking into your body and the umbilical cord sent nutrients, oxygen and blood into the womb before carrying the old blood cells out. I was eating for you, but soon you would eat on your own.

When I pressed on my belly, you swam away. When your hand or foot passed your mouth, your forehead wrinkled, your lips moved out and you tried to suck.

In week Fourteen, your skin was still thin; your bones and blood vessels showed through.

Your little kidneys began to function and you worked hard to swallow and pass the amniotic fluid you swam in. Your body burped and hiccupped as it got used to drinking. You were now the size of a softball.

> "My frame was not hidden from you, when I was being made in secret, intricately woven in the depths of the earth. Your eyes saw my unformed substance." Psalm 139:15, 16a

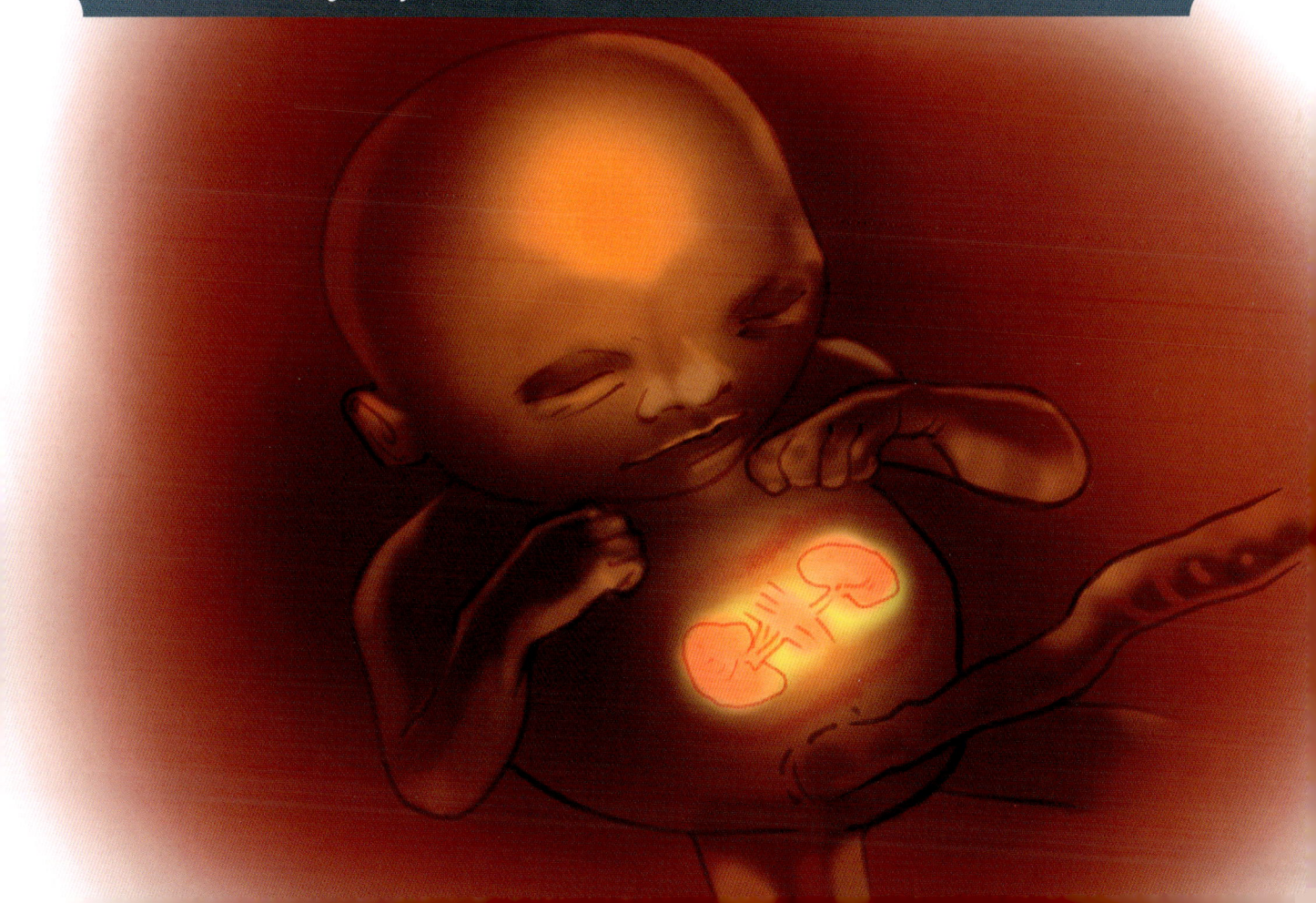

In week Fifteen, you grew eyebrows and eyelids. The hair on your head grew thicker and became colored. Your little brain, muscles and nerves were all connected.

You loved to suck your thumb and grab the fingers of your other hand. It felt like I had a little butterfly in my belly… but I knew it was you!

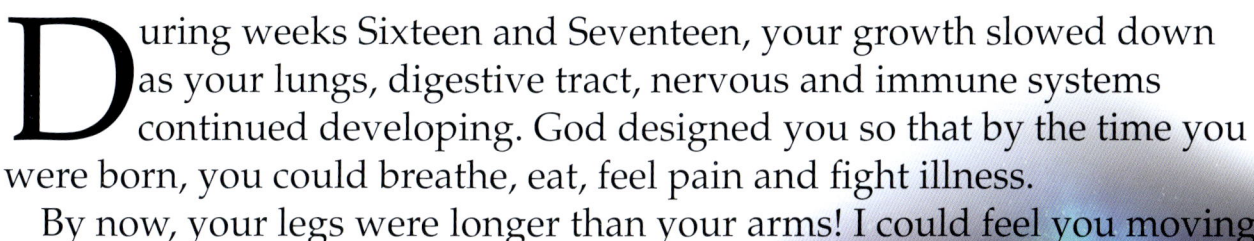

During weeks Sixteen and Seventeen, your growth slowed down as your lungs, digestive tract, nervous and immune systems continued developing. God designed you so that by the time you were born, you could breathe, eat, feel pain and fight illness.

By now, your legs were longer than your arms! I could feel you moving and everyone could see that you were growing inside of me.

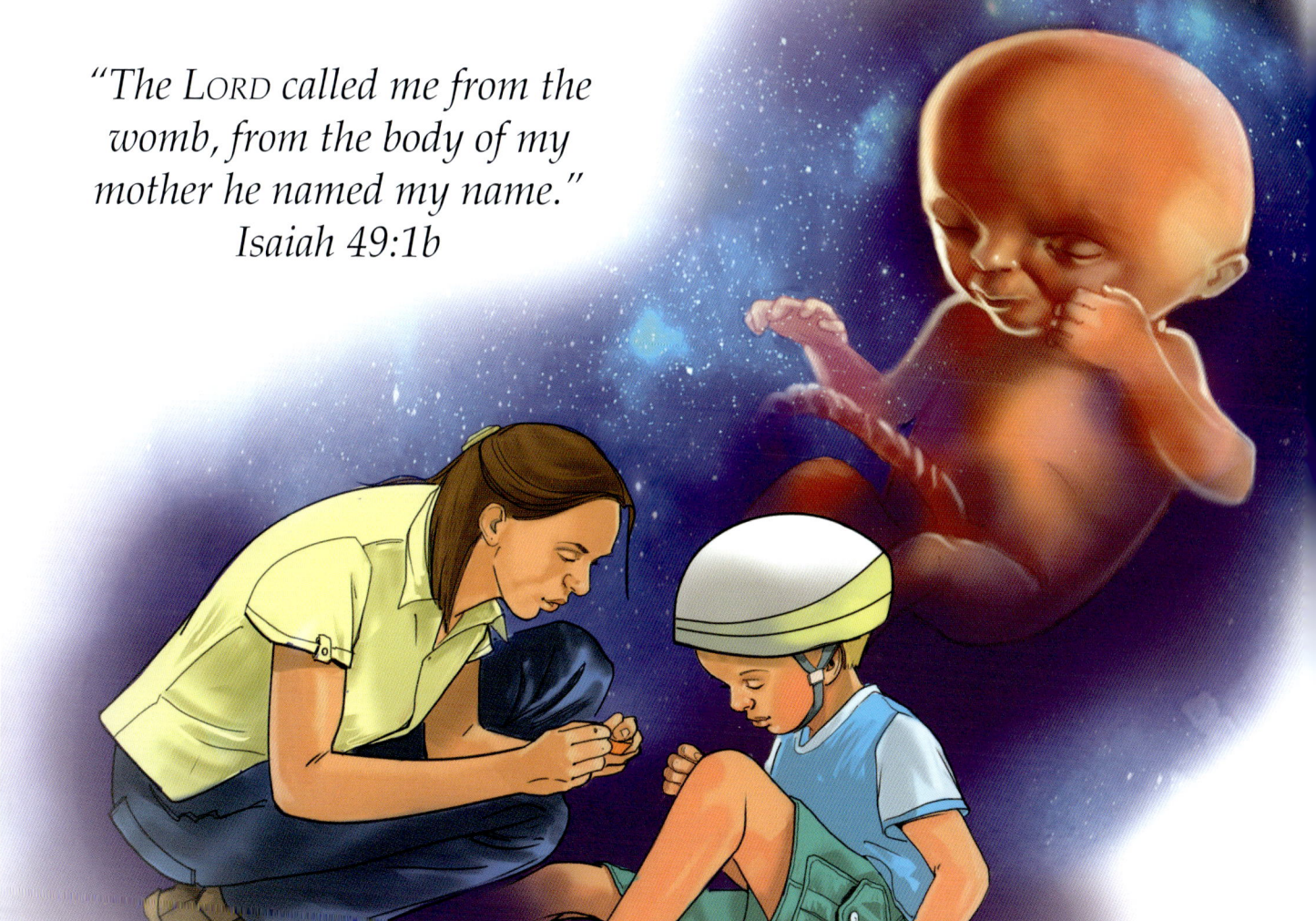

*"The Lord called me from the womb, from the body of my mother he named my name."*
*Isaiah 49:1b*

In week Eighteen, you were very active, twisting, somersaulting, grabbing and stretching. Your eyeballs moved up, down and around. There was nothing to eat in my belly, but your taste buds could tell the difference between sweet and sour. You had a full set of baby teeth under your gums.

By weeks Nineteen and Twenty, you weighed half a pound. You stuck out your little tongue and pulled it back in. Now you could hear my heart beating, my blood rushing in my veins and the music I was listening to. You heard Dad's voice – and mine. Loud noises scared you.

I had an ultrasound to see you. You were so amazing; I couldn't believe I would have to wait another twenty weeks before I could hold you.

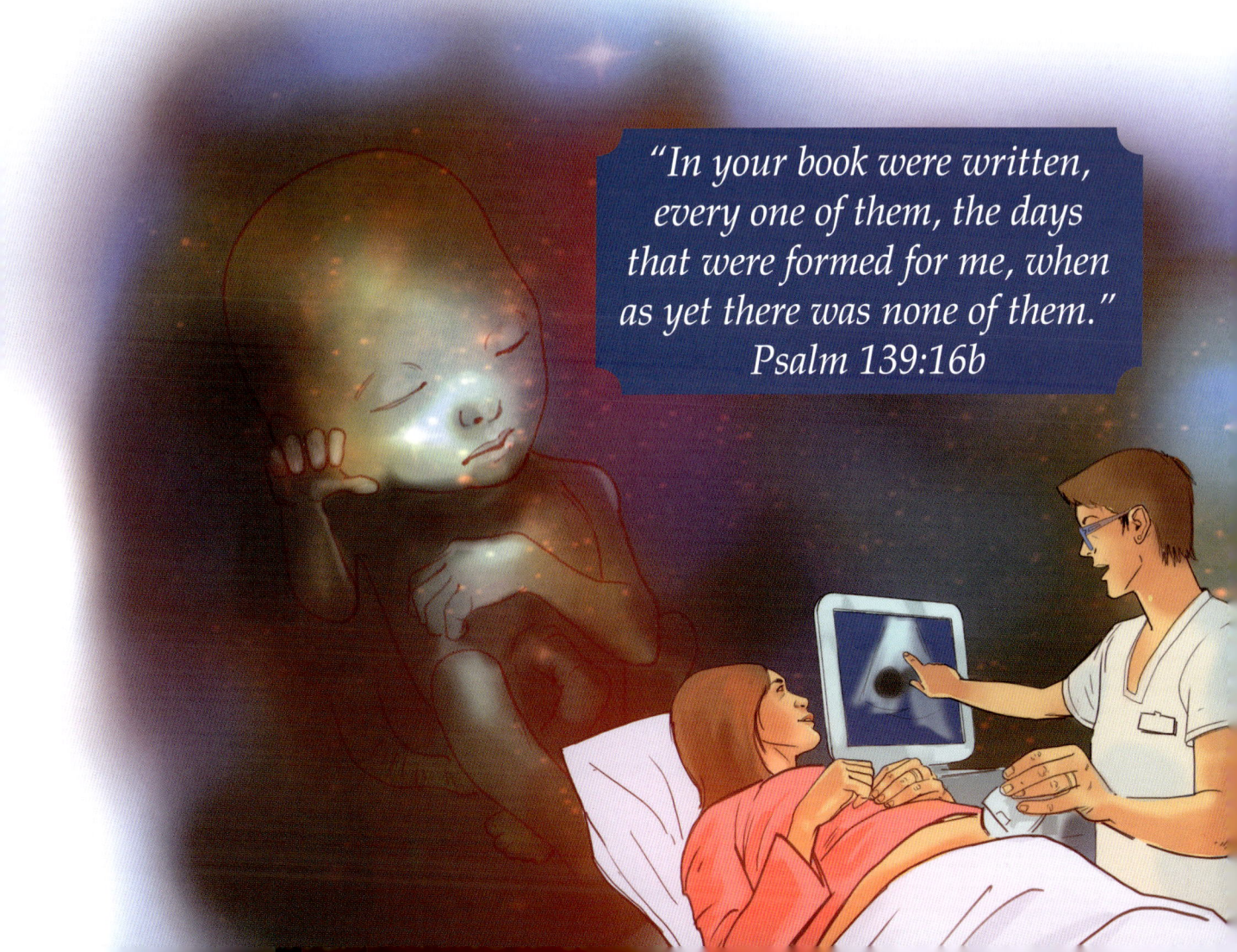

> "In your book were written, every one of them, the days that were formed for me, when as yet there was none of them."
> Psalm 139:16b

You were finally starting to gain fat so you could stay warm. In week Twenty-one, you were the size of a large banana. By week Twenty-three, you were the size of a small doll and weighed a pound.

You grew finger and toeprints, and your skin was covered in a white waxy coating. God protected you from absorbing too much amniotic fluid and from being scratched by your growing fingernails.

As you breathed amniotic fluid in and out of your lungs, you developed more sacs for the air you would soon be breathing.

*"For everything created by God is good..."* 1 Timothy 4:4a

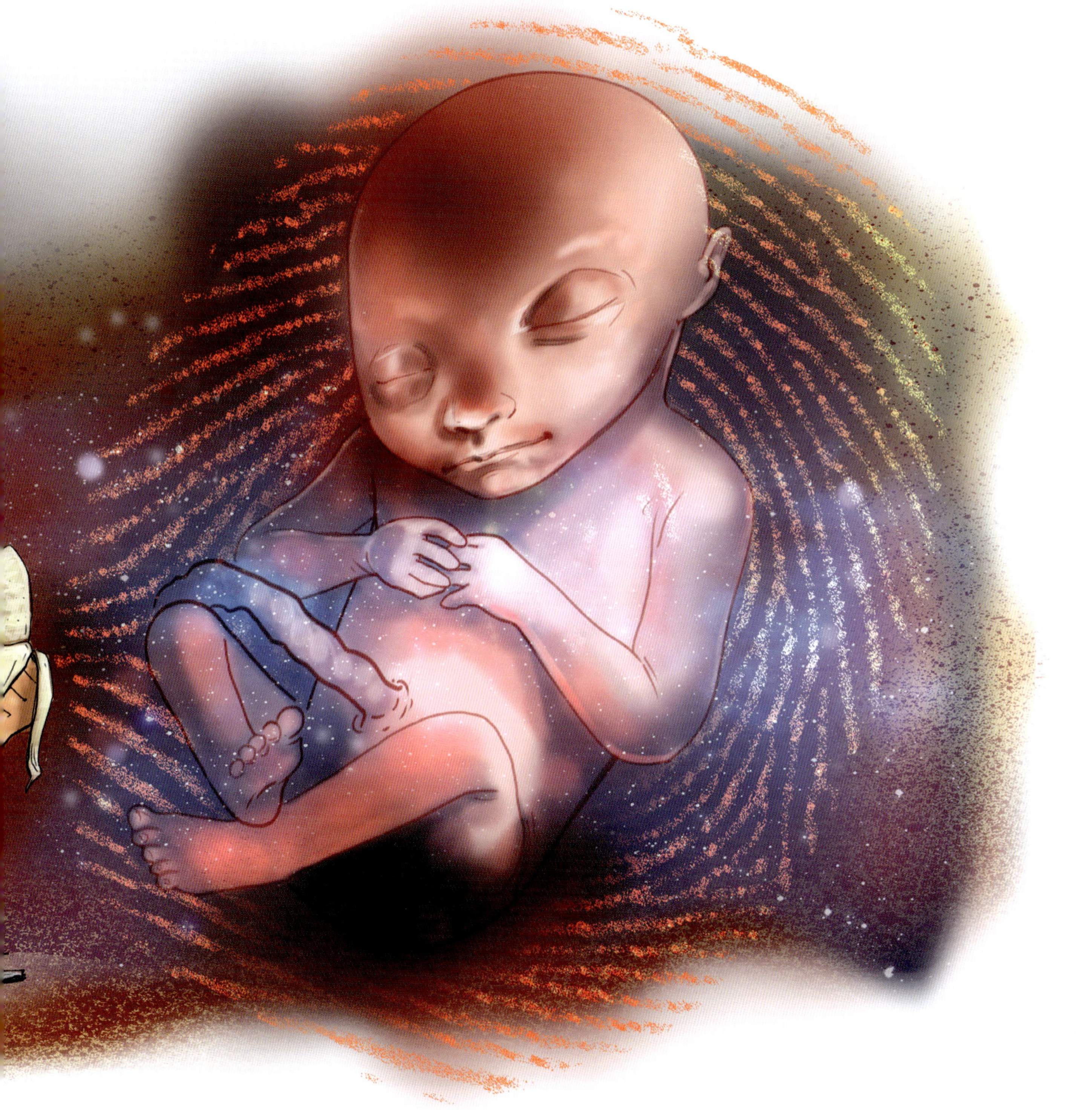

Now your brain was growing quickly. In weeks Twenty-four and Twenty-five, you could tell the difference between my voice and Dad's. You could remember music and you were opening and closing your eyes. You slept and woke, not always when I hoped you would.

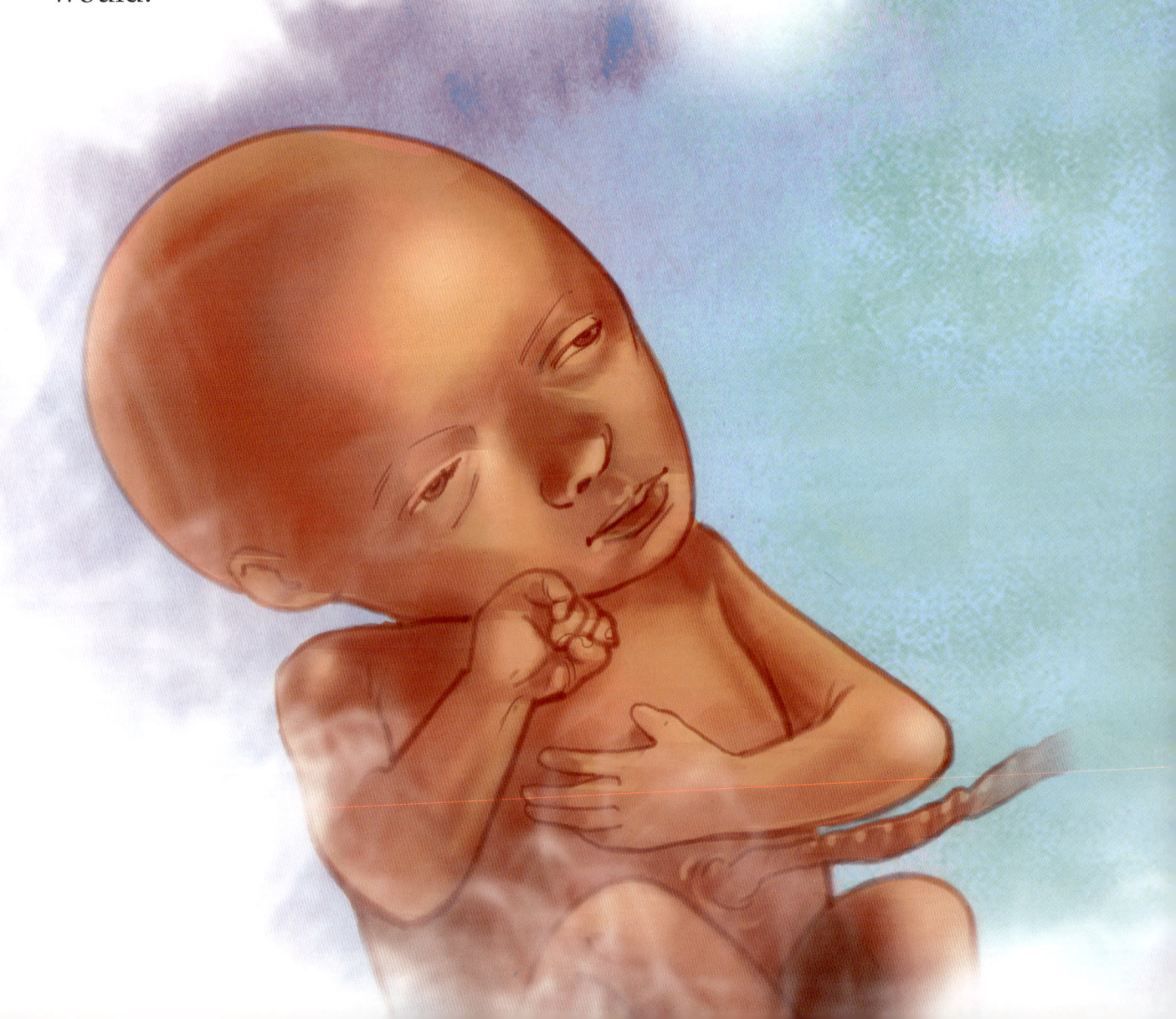

You weren't ready to be born yet, but some babies who are born in these weeks live with a lot of help from doctors, nurses and the hospital.

*"…for you created all things, and by your will they existed and were created."* Revelation 4:11b

By week Twenty-six, you weighed two pounds. Sitting, you were almost ten inches long.

The fine hair covering your body started to fall off. Eyelashes, eyebrows, fingernails and toenails were growing. The hair on your head was getting thicker and longer.

You could see six to eight inches away. You spent a lot of time examining your hands and feet!

Your vocal cords were working by week Twenty-seven. You wouldn't cry until the day you were born, but since then, you haven't stopped using them!

You didn't have any toys in my belly, so you pulled on the strong umbilical cord and pushed your feet against the womb. Sometimes I could see the shape of your foot or your elbow against my skin. Once in a while, you kicked me hard in the ribs.

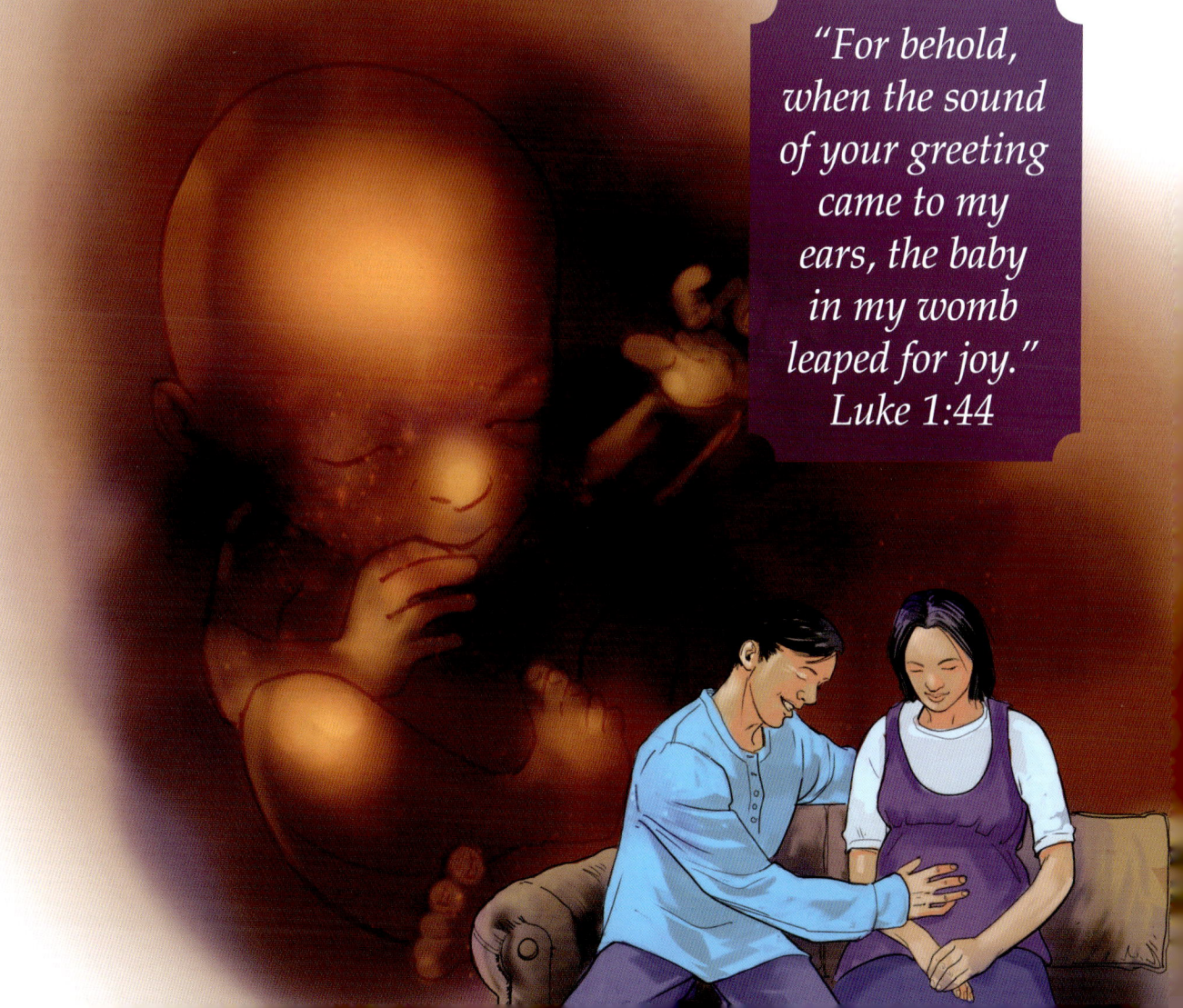

> "For behold, when the sound of your greeting came to my ears, the baby in my womb leaped for joy."
> Luke 1:44

By week Twenty-eight you began to dream. I wonder what you were dreaming about, little one? I know I was dreaming of you. What would you look like? Who would you be? What would it feel like to hold you?

"*...God, the L*ORD*, who created the heavens and stretched them out, who spread out the earth and what comes from it, who gives breath to the people on it and spirit to those who walk in it..." Isaiah 42:5b*

In weeks Twenty-nine and Thirty, you grew to be three pounds. You sat almost as tall as a ruler.

God was using this time in my womb to help you gain weight and to let your lungs grow and mature. You grew new little air sacs in your lungs. They became coated in a slippery material called surfactant that let them blow up like a balloon; you wouldn't have enough until week Thirty-five.

By now, your immune system was ready to fight colds. Your brain was growing and beginning to wrinkle and fold so that it could fit inside your skull.

*"Your hands have made and fashioned me; give me understanding that I may learn your commandments." Psalm 119:73*

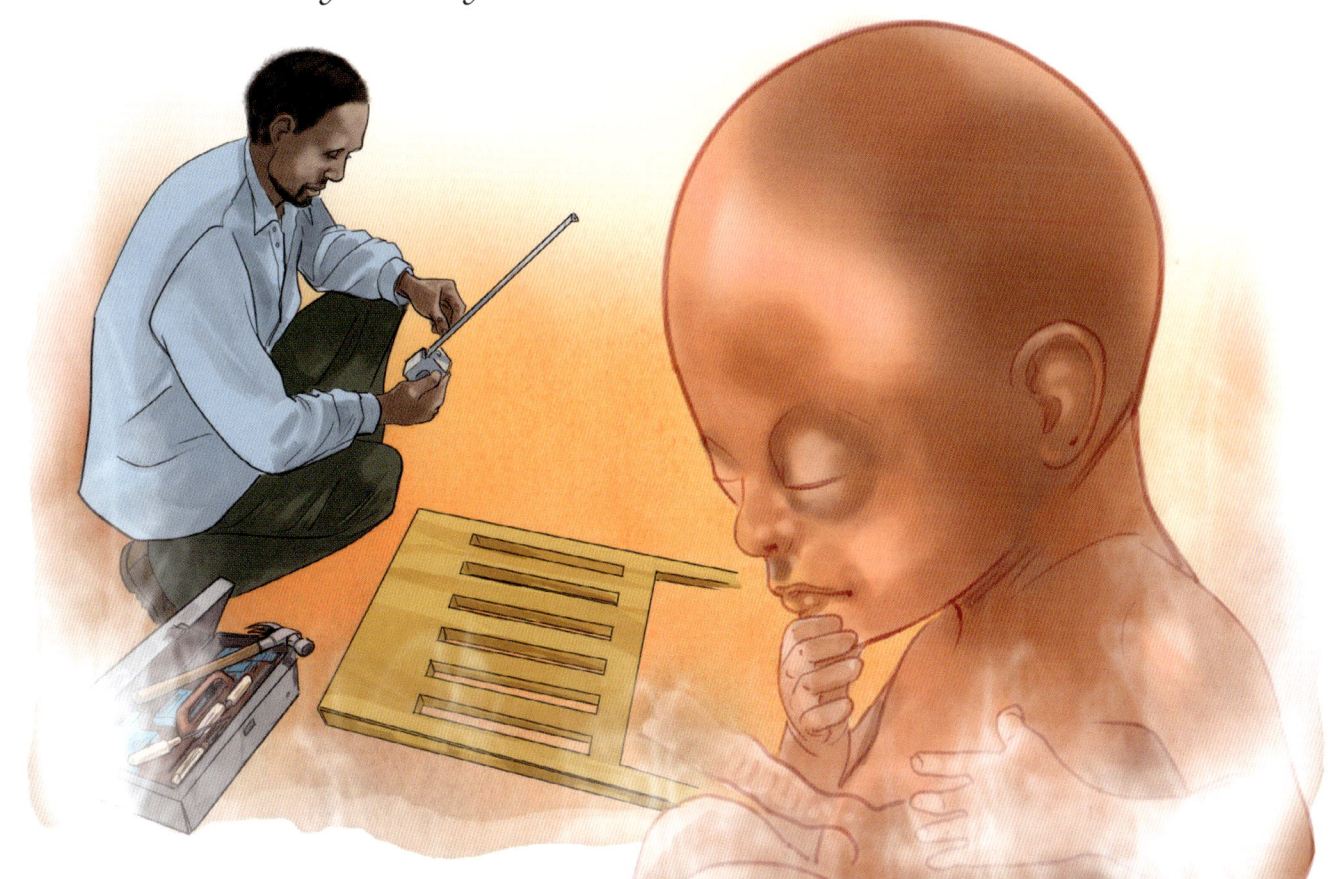

My child, between week Thirty-one and week Thirty-six you were busy gaining weight. Sometimes you gained more than half a pound each week.

By week Thirty-six you were about six pounds. You were getting heavy, and I was starting to get tired!

Your lungs began to function. Your brain grew and grew, and your digestive system was ready for milk.

At the beginning of this time, you were still somersaulting, twisting and turning. You should have seen the funny shapes my stomach became!

By the end, there wasn't much room for you to move. You stretched and you pushed.

*" Yet you are he who took me from the womb; you made me trust you at my mother's breasts." Psalm 22:9*

Most of the time, God puts just one baby in the womb. That baby is there all alone. Sometimes, God places two babies in the same womb. Once in a great while, he forms three or more babies together. These babies spend a long time very close to each other. It is a precious time and they are often good friends later in life.

Twins and triplets are usually born several weeks early. They just run out of room to grow!

*"For we are his workmanship…"*
*Ephesians 2:10a*

The last three weeks in my womb, you gained weight; about one and a half pounds altogether.

Your organs were almost ready for life outside my womb. Your lungs were the last organ to finish growing and this time was very important to your breathing.

There were no more somersaults, but you enjoyed twisting. It was a strange feeling for me.

*"Let them praise the name of the Lord! For he commanded and they were created." Psalm 148:5*

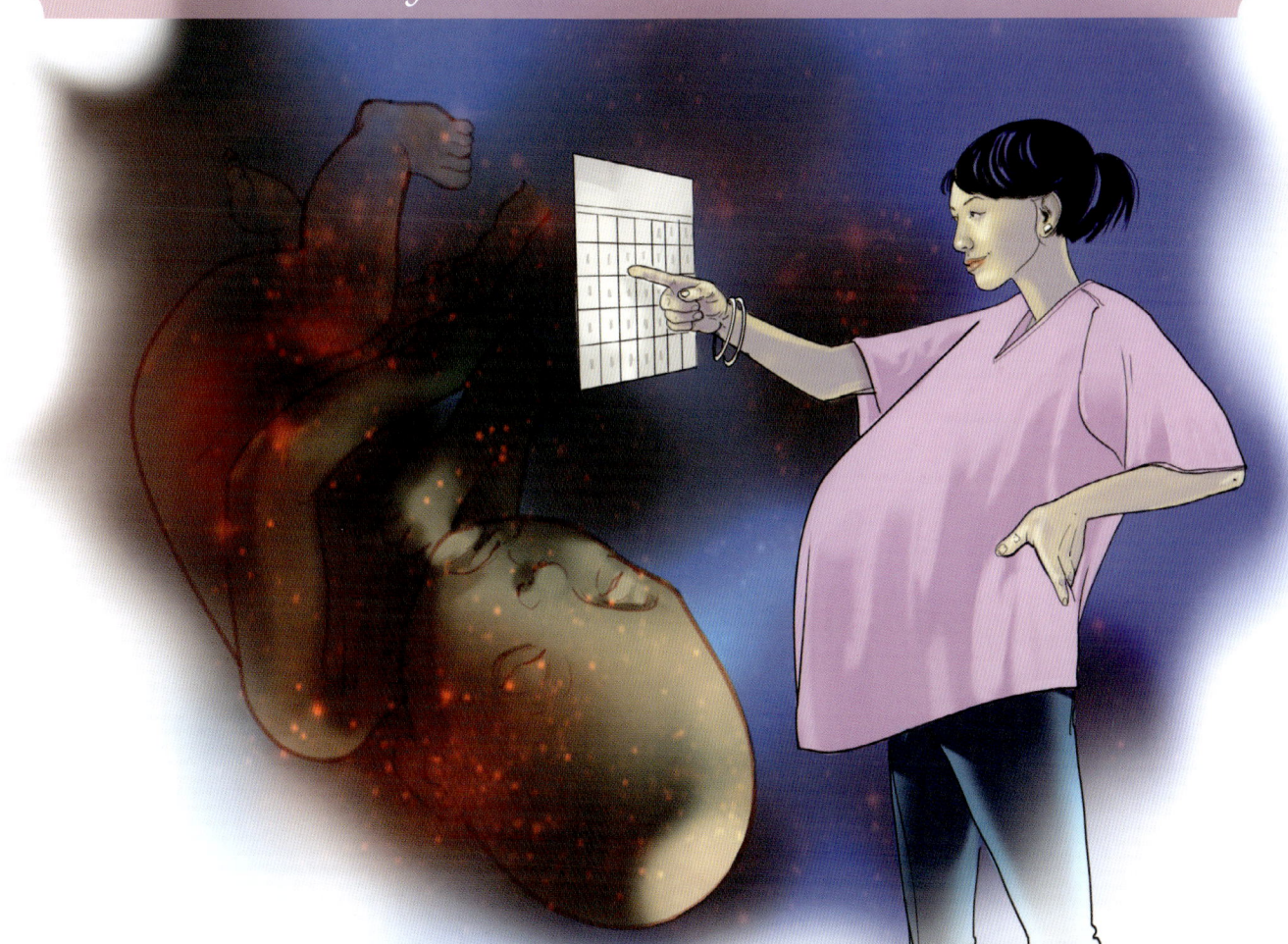

The day you were born was one of the most exciting of my life! Though it was difficult and painful for both of us, it was such a joy to see your face. I counted your fingers and kissed your precious nose.

God had a plan for your life, long before even I was born. You are special and you were created for a purpose.

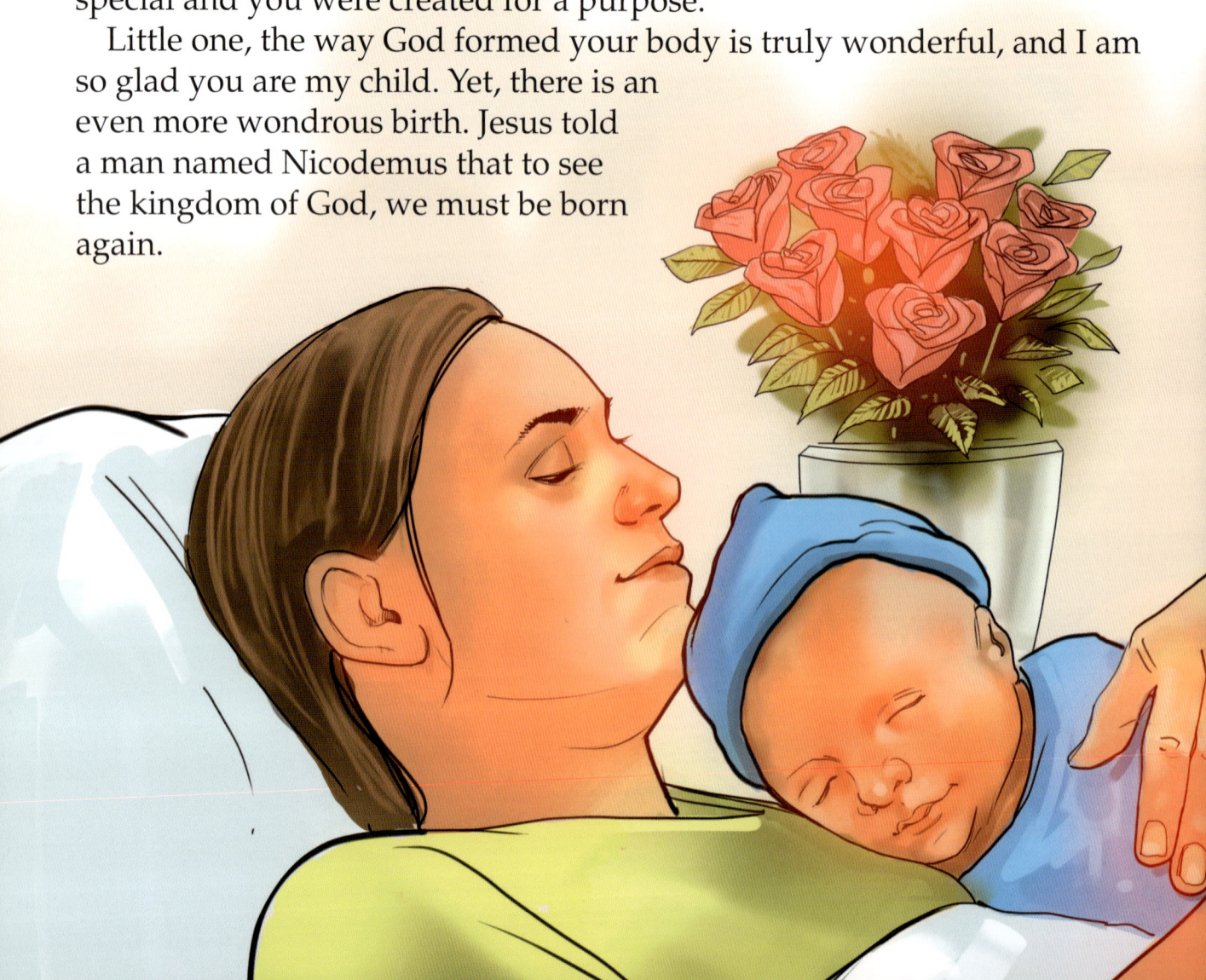

Little one, the way God formed your body is truly wonderful, and I am so glad you are my child. Yet, there is an even more wondrous birth. Jesus told a man named Nicodemus that to see the kingdom of God, we must be born again.

Now you know how your body was born, let me tell you how your spirit can be reborn.

*"Upon you I have leaned from before my birth; you are he who took me from my mother's womb. My praise is continually of you."*
*Psalm 71:6*

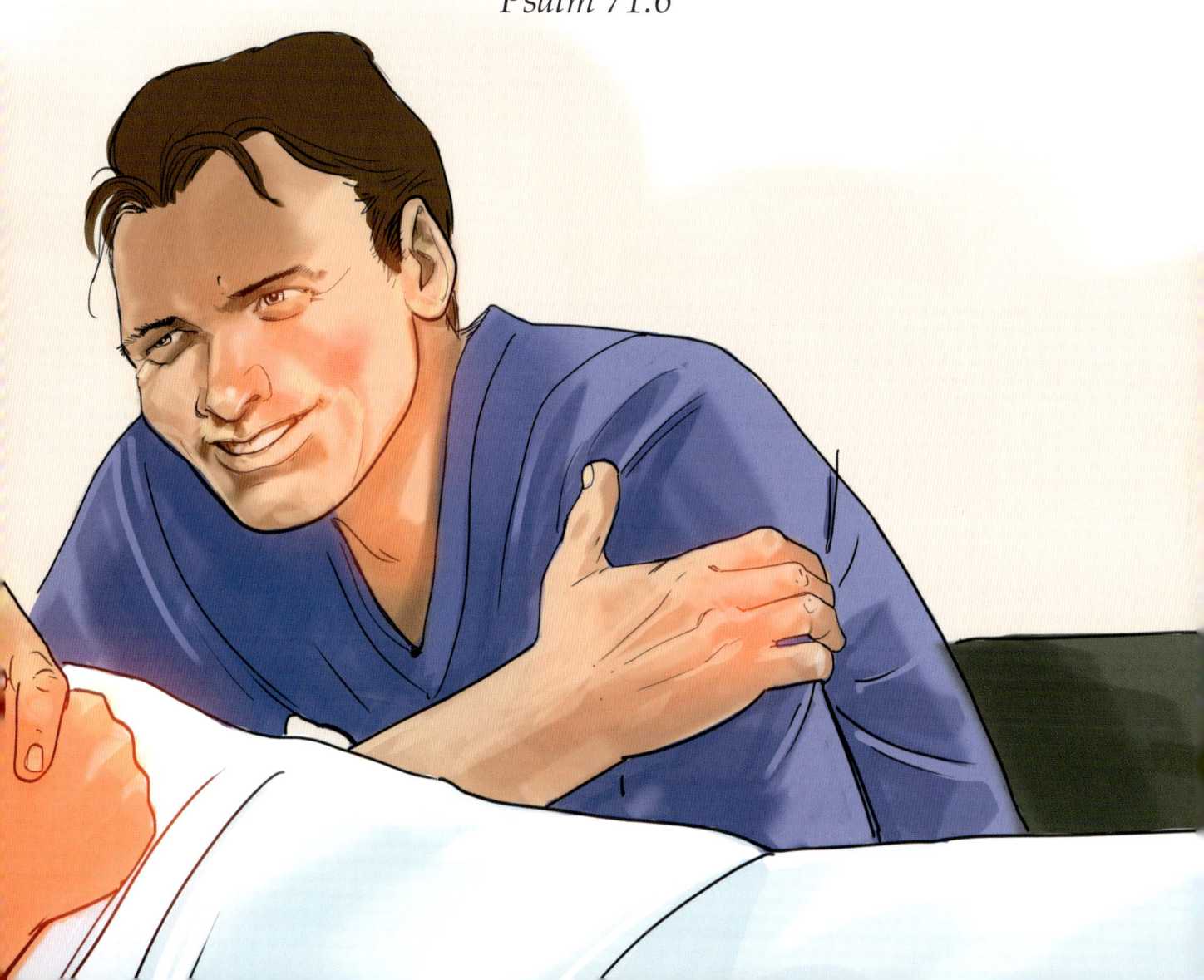

Child, we have all done wrong things in the eyes of our Creator. He calls these wrong actions sin and they separate us from him. Our sin deserves punishment. But God made a way for us to become his children. God sent his only Son, Jesus, to take our punishment on the cross. Jesus died, was resurrected, and will one day return for his children. My precious one, you can be reborn if you repent of your sin. This means you are to turn away from doing wrong. Trust that Jesus Christ is the only one who can save you from the punishment your sin deserves. If you trust in Christ, you are adopted by God as his very own child, and you are born again a second time—this time in spirit. Live your life for Jesus!

*"According to his great mercy, he has caused us to be born again to a living hope through the resurrection of Jesus Christ from the dead..."* 1 Peter 1:3b

## BIBLIOGRAPHY: WONDERFULLY MADE

Bryan, Jenny. *The Miracle of Birth*. Wilton: Victoria House Publishing, 1994.

Curtis, Dr. Glade B., OB/GYN and Schuler, Judith, M.S. *Your Pregnancy Week by Week*. Cambridge: Da Capo Press, 2004.

Murkoff, Heidi, Eisenberg, Arlene and Hathaway, Sandee, BSN. *What to Expect When You're Expecting*. New York: Workman Publishing Company, 2002.

Regan, Lesley, M.D. *I'm Pregnant! A Week-by-Week Guide from Conception to Birth*. New York: DK Publishing, Inc., 2005.

MATERNITY

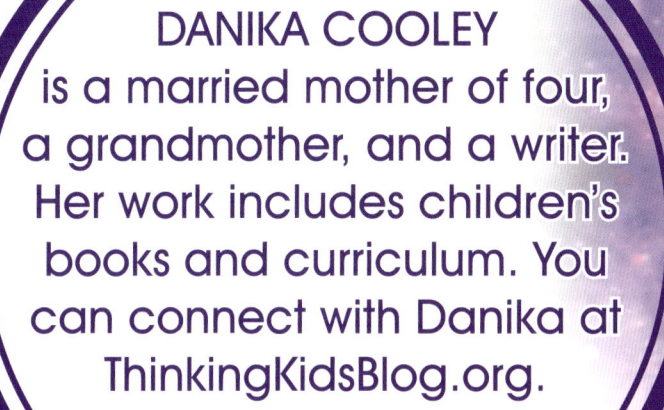

**DANIKA COOLEY** is a married mother of four, a grandmother, and a writer. Her work includes children's books and curriculum. You can connect with Danika at ThinkingKidsBlog.org.

**JEFF ANDERSON** is a Christian freelance artist based in the North East of England. He has over thirty years of experience working in publishing, comics and graphic novels.

# CHRISTIAN FOCUS PUBLICATIONS

Christian Focus Publications publishes books for adults and children under its four main imprints: Christian Focus, CF4K, Mentor and Christian Heritage. Our books reflect our conviction that God's Word is reliable and Jesus is the way to know him, and live for ever with him. Our children's list includes a Sunday School curriculum that covers pre-school to early teens, and puzzle and activity books. We also publish personal and family devotional titles, biographies and inspirational stories that children will love.

If you are looking for quality Bible teaching for children then we have an excellent range of Bible stories and age-specific theological books. From pre-school board books to teenage apologetics, we have it covered!

**CF4•K**
*Because you're never too young to know Jesus*